THIS JOURNAL BELONGS TO:

....

....

Made in the USA
Coppell, TX
03 December 2023

25223258R00066